Commissioned and first performed by Sebastian Thomson at St Paul's Cathedral on 24 October 2010
as part of 'The Angel of Creation Commissions'

Rhapsody

Manuals coupled throughout

DAVID BEDNALL

Molto maestoso

OXFORD UNIVERSITY PRESS, MUSIC DEPARTMENT, GREAT CLARENDON STREET, OXFORD OX2 6DP

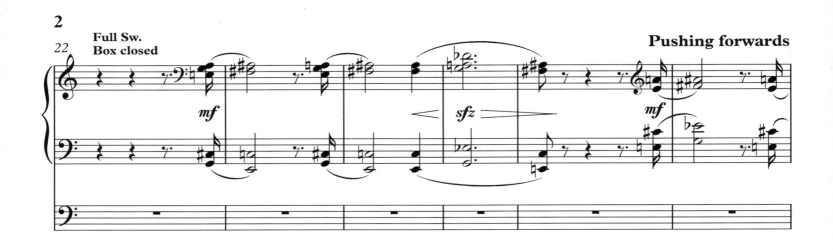

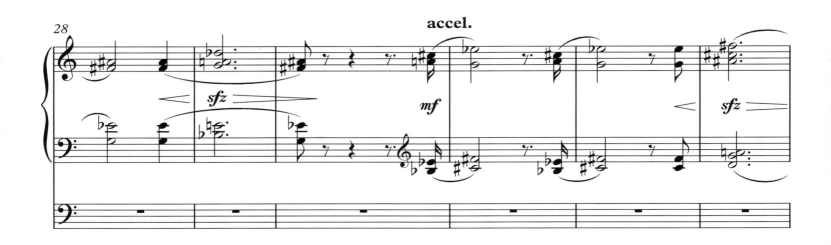

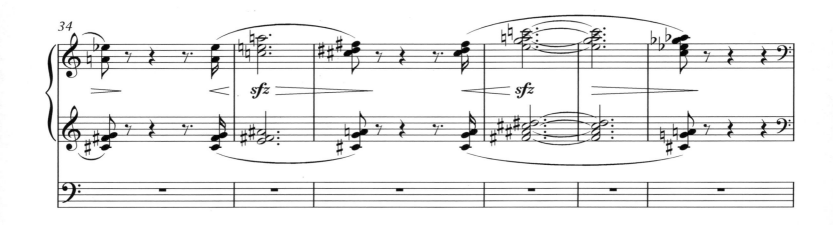

4

Turbulent—fairly fast and with great drive

A little slower and more tranquil
Straight on under echo

+ Foundations 4'

Turbulent—as before

Grave

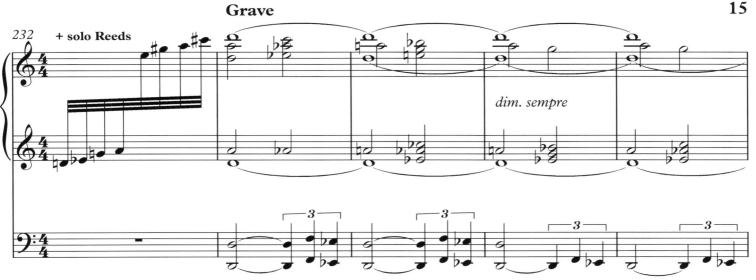

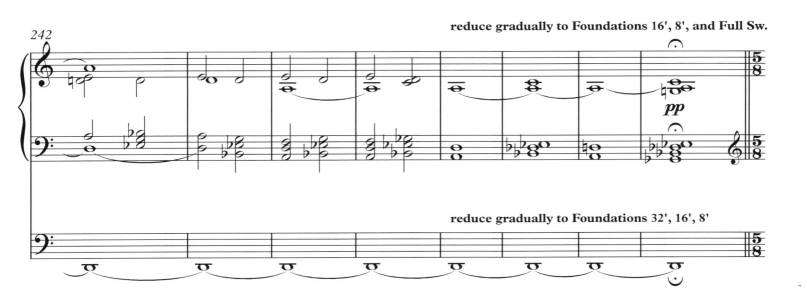

Fast and driving—as before

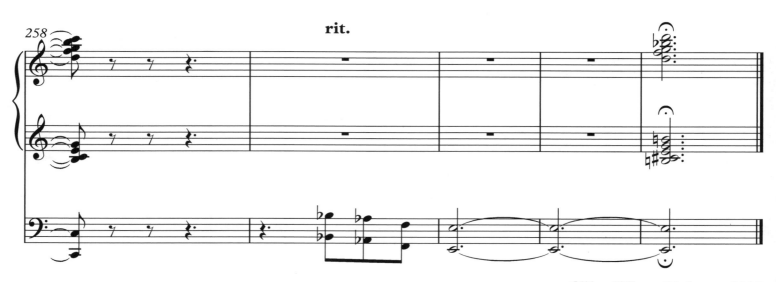

Clifton Village, 18 August 2010